I0813178

ENGINEERING ANSWERS

How Skyscrapers Stand Tall

BY LIBBY WILSON

An Imprint of Abdo Publishing
abdobooks.com

abdobooks.com

Printed in the United States of America, North Mankato, Minnesota.
102024
012025

Cover Photo: Shutterstock Images
Interior Photos: Shutterstock Images, 4–5, 18, 26; Pandora Pictures/Shutterstock Images, 7; Semmick Photo/Shutterstock Images, 8; Laura Kick/Shutterstock Images, 10; Michael Doolittle/Alamy, 12–13; Jeff Greenberg/Universal Images Group/Getty Images, 14; Dorling Kindersley/Dorling Kindersley RF/Getty Images, 17; Philip Openshaw/Shutterstock Images, 20–21; Gary Hershorn/Corbis News/Getty Images, 22; John Henshall/Alamy, 25; Apidet Saengwoorachot/Shutterstock Images, 28; Beata Zawrzel/NurPhoto/Getty Images, 29

Editor: Marley Richmond
Series Designer: Laura Kuchar

Library of Congress Control Number: 2024938389

Publisher's Cataloging-in-Publication Data

Names: Wilson, Libby, author.
Title: How skyscrapers stand tall / by Libby Wilson
Description: Minneapolis, Minnesota: ABDO Publishing, 2025 | Series: Engineering answers | Includes online resources and index.
Identifiers: ISBN 9781098295899 (lib. bdg.) | ISBN 9798384916895 (ebook)
Subjects: LCSH: Engineering--Juvenile literature. | Skyscrapers--Juvenile literature. | High-rise buildings--Juvenile literature. | Architectural engineering--Juvenile literature. | Questions and answers--Juvenile literature. | Engineering design--Juvenile literature.
Classification: DDC 620.1--dc23

CONTENTS

The Burj Khalifa opened in January 2010. It took six years to build.

CHAPTER 1

An Engineering Marvel

A group of visitors steps into a shiny elevator. They are in the Burj Khalifa, a skyscraper in Dubai, United Arab Emirates. The Burj Khalifa stretches 2,717 feet (828 m) into the air. That is more than half a mile (0.8 km) up.

This skyscraper is the tallest human-made object on Earth.

The elevator brings the visitors toward the top story. They travel 33 feet per second (10 m/s). The floors they pass hold hotel rooms, offices, and apartments. The skyscraper also has stores, a library, and five swimming pools. The building can hold 35,000 people at one time.

The visitors exit at floor 148. They step onto the world's highest outdoor observation deck. People look in awe at the city far below.

Some visitors feel the building **sway**. Like all skyscrapers, the Burj Khalifa is always moving. Weather, winds, and a shifting **foundation** constantly affect it. During storms, winds around the skyscraper can reach up to 150 miles per

The Burj Khalifa has 163 floors. Floors 124, 125, and 148 are built for people to look out over the city from the skyscraper.

hour (240 km/h). The top of the building can sway up to 6 feet (2.6 m). Visitors may wonder how such a tall building stays up.

Many large cities are known for their skylines. People may recognize the unique skyscrapers that stand tallest in a city.

What Is a Skyscraper?

A building that is 490 feet (150 m) or taller is a skyscraper. At least half its space must be usable by people. This includes homes and offices. Structures such as cell towers do not count.

Every year, many people move to big cities. But cities are already crowded. Tall buildings can create space for new people.

World's First Steel Skyscraper

Stone was a common material for early buildings. But steel is much lighter. The Home Insurance Building in Chicago was the world's first skyscraper. It was made from steel. The building weighed one-third as much as it would have if made of stone.

The steel skeleton is often the first part of a skyscraper that is built.

Stone Structures to Steel Skeletons

People have long been fascinated by large structures. Long ago, Egyptians built stone pyramids. Europeans built stone cathedrals. But stone couldn't be used for today's tall skyscrapers. It is too heavy. The stone would collapse under its own weight.

In the mid-1800s, **engineers** started making long steel beams. These beams support much more weight than stone. They are also lighter and take up less space. Builders began to use beams to create steel **skeletons** inside tall structures. Buildings could finally stretch into the sky.

Explore Online

Visit the website below. Does it give any new information about skyscrapers that wasn't in Chapter One?

Where Is the Tallest Building?

abdocorelibrary.com/skyscrapers-stand-tall

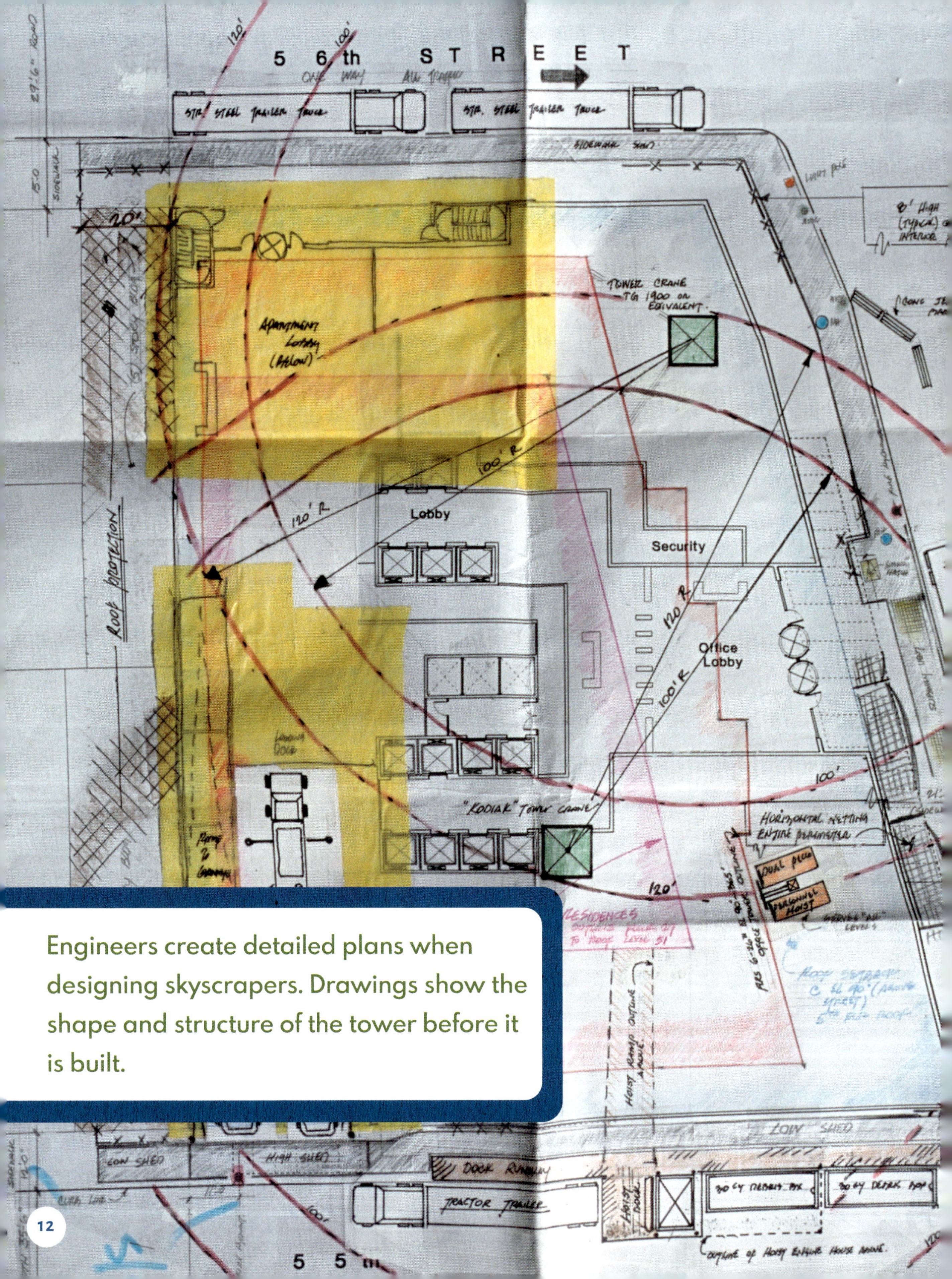

Engineers create detailed plans when designing skyscrapers. Drawings show the shape and structure of the tower before it is built.

CHAPTER 2

Stable Buildings

Skyscrapers stand tall because engineers and **architects** design them to be **stable**. A stable building must support its own weight. This weight is called the dead load. Dead load never changes.

Skyscrapers around the world experience forces from different kinds of weather. In some cities, skyscrapers must withstand hurricanes.

Buildings must also support their live load. Live load is always changing. It includes weight added to the structure, such as furniture and people. Live load also includes **forces** such as those from wind, snow, and earthquakes.

These forces include compression, tension, torsion, and shear. Compression is a squeezing force. The weight of snow on a roof squeezes the floors below. This creates compression. Tension is the opposite. It is a stretching force. A skyscraper that bends in strong winds experiences tension.

Earthquakes cause torsion and shear. Torsion is a twisting force. Shear causes parts of a material to slide past one another in opposite directions.

The loads and forces on tall structures are extreme. Just the dead load can be several hundred thousand tons. Skyscrapers manage live and dead loads by transferring them into their foundations.

Into the Ground

A foundation is the bottom part of a building that connects it to the ground. A skyscraper's foundation goes deep into the earth to support the structure. This is similar to how roots anchor a tall tree.

An Unwelcome Surprise

Engineers drilled 400 holes into the ground where Malaysia's Petronas Towers were going to be built. They found solid rock near the surface in some areas. But the rock sloped sharply downward in other places. Such uneven ground wouldn't support the heavy towers. Engineers had to choose another building site.

How Skyscrapers Handle Loads

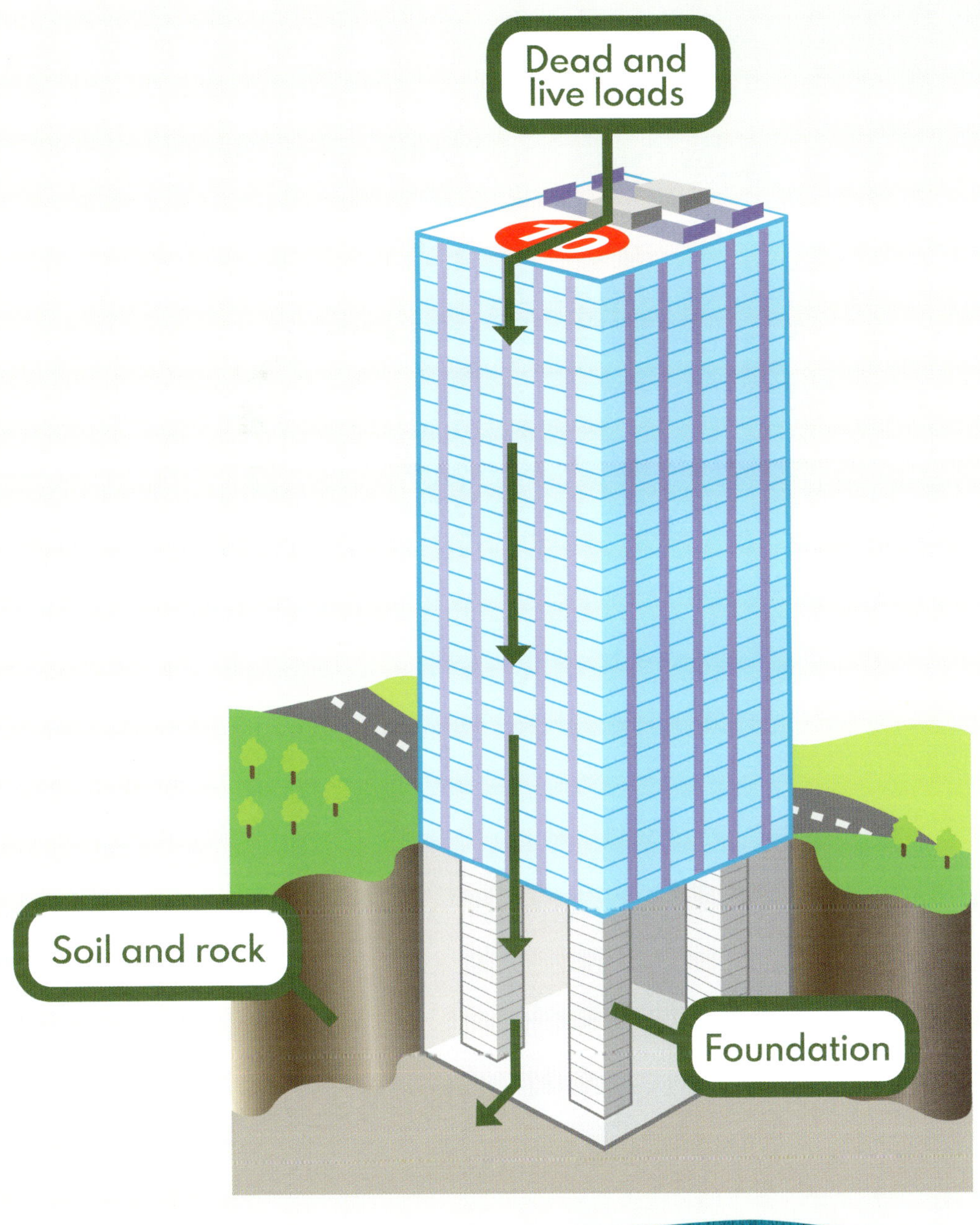

A skyscraper's skeleton transfers its loads into the foundation. The foundation spreads the loads into the ground. The force of the earth keeps the skyscraper stable.

Piles are pounded deep into the ground by pile-driving machines. Piles support the foundation of the skyscraper.

When wind pushes against a skyscraper, the building's foundation pushes against the earth. The ground is strong and hard. It keeps the skyscraper stable. When snow piles on a roof, the skyscraper's skeleton carries the extra weight deep into the earth. The weight is supported by the solid ground.

Engineers study the ground where a skyscraper is to be built. They test how stable the soil is. They measure the distance to solid rock.

Many skyscraper foundations are built with piles. Piles are long posts. They reach deep into the ground and keep a skyscraper standing strong. Piles are often made of reinforced concrete. This is concrete strengthened with steel bars. The Burj Khalifa sits on 192 piles. Each is 164 feet (50 m) long and 5 feet (1.5 m) across. The ground below China's Shanghai Tower is not as stable. The tower sits on 980 piles.

Further Evidence

Watch the video below. Does it give any new evidence to support Chapter Two?

Structural Forces

abdocorelibrary.com/skyscrapers-stand-tall

Concrete cores rise through the center of many skyscrapers.

CHAPTER 3

Into the Sky

Wind is often faster and stronger high up in the sky. Tall structures experience more force from wind than short buildings. Skyscrapers often face 100-mile-per-hour (161-km/h) winds. Many skyscrapers have concrete cores to resist the wind.

In New York City, 432 Park Avenue is a skyscraper with several stories left empty. The building's core shows through these open stories.

These cores strengthen buildings. Inside many skyscrapers, concrete cores house the building's elevators and stairs.

Other skyscrapers use **exterior** braces for strength. The John Hancock Center in Chicago, Illinois, faces powerful winds from Lake Michigan. The outside of the building has a series of stacked steel *X*'s. These make the building strong and stable.

Some skyscrapers have stories that are completely open. Wind blows right through them. This design reduces the amount of wind that could rock the building.

Tapering a tower lessens wind forces. This means a structure gets narrower as it rises. The Willis Tower in Chicago is made of nine tubes. Only two of the tubes reach the top. The others stop at different levels. The tapered building breaks up wind flow.

The Burj Khalifa's shape resists strong desert winds. It is built in a tripod structure around a center core. It has three wings that support the core and each other. This type of support is called buttressing.

Architects design skyscrapers to be flexible. Flexibility allows a building to sway. But too much motion can damage the building. It might

Metal-Coated Glass

Skyscraper glass must be strong enough to withstand high winds. Glass can be coated with thin layers of metal to make it stronger. Each coat is a thousand times thinner than a human hair. This high-tech glass withstands hurricane-force winds.

Taipei 101 is a skyscraper in Taiwan. The building's tuned mass damper helped the skyscraper stay strong during a 2015 typhoon with winds up to 145 miles per hour (233 km/h).

also make people feel seasick. Equipment can be installed to dampen or lessen the sway. These are called tuned mass dampers. Some dampers are metal balls hung inside upper floors. They swing to counter the swaying motion.

Computer programs allow engineers to see how different designs will affect a skyscraper's stability before the structure is built.

Modern technology has greatly improved skyscraper stability. Engineers use computers to plan a structure before it is built. They can see exactly how forces will affect it. Computers also help manage an existing building. They monitor the forces affecting a skyscraper and the stability of its structure. New technology allows skyscrapers to stand tall in cities all over the world.

Primary Source

George Efstathiou was an architect who helped design the Burj Khalifa. He said:

> When the skyscrapers reach this height, the most dangerous and unpredictable element is wind. . . . When the wind blows on the side of the skyscraper, it definitely tends to bend the skyscraper trying to push it over.

Source: Hobbes S. Sujith. "How Peter Irvin, a Renowned Wind Engineering Expert, Saved Burj Khalifa from the Wind." *CIRIA*, n.d., ciria.org. Accessed 19 Apr. 2024.

What's the Big Idea?

Read this quote carefully. What is its main idea? Explain how the main idea is supported by the details.

Engineering Facts

Compression

Tension

Torsion

Shear

Dead load includes the floors, windows, and structure of a skyscraper.
Live load includes the people and furniture inside a skyscraper.

Glossary

architect
a person who is trained to design buildings

engineers
people who are trained to design and build machines and structures

exterior
on the outside

force
a push or pull that transfers energy into an object

foundation
the bottom part of a structure that connects it to the ground

skeleton
a strong structure that supports a building or living thing

stable
not likely to fall or fail

sway
to rock back and forth

Online Resources

To learn more about skyscrapers, visit our free resource websites below.

Visit **abdocorelibrary.com** or scan this QR code for free Common Core resources for teachers and students, including vetted activities, multimedia, and booklinks, for deeper subject comprehension.

Visit **abdobooklinks.com** or scan this QR code for free additional online weblinks for further learning. These links are routinely monitored and updated to provide the most current information available.

Learn More

Mattern, Joanne. *How Bridges Stand Strong*. Abdo, 2025.

Miller, Derek. *The STEM of Skyscrapers.* Cavendish Square, 2021.

Vonder Brink, Tracy. *Skyscrapers.* Crabtree, 2024.

Index

About the Author

Libby Wilson loves researching and writing nonfiction books for kids. She delights in finding facts that make her say, "Wow!" Wilson lives in Pennsylvania and North Carolina with her husband and their golden retriever.